Easy Irish Cookbook

The Effortless Chef Series

By
Chef Maggie Chow

Published by
BookSumo, a division of Saxonberg Associates
http://www.booksumo.com/

A Gift From Me To You...

Send the Book!

I know you like easy cooking. But what about Japanese Sushi?

Join my private reader's club and get a copy of ***Infinite Sushi: A Complete Set of Sushi and Japanese Recipes*** by fellow BookSumo author Hashimoto Kazuma for FREE!

Send the Book!

Enjoy some of the best sushi available!

You will also receive updates about all my new books when they are free. So please show your support.

Also don't forget to like and subscribe on the social networks. I love meeting my readers. Links to all my profiles are below so please click and connect :)

Facebook

Twitter

ABOUT THE AUTHOR.

Maggie Chow is the author and creator of your favorite *Easy Cookbooks* and *The Effortless Chef Series*. Maggie is a lover of all things related to food. Maggie loves nothing more than finding new recipes, trying them out, and then making them her own, by adding or removing ingredients, tweaking cooking times, and anything to make the recipe not only taste better, but be easier to cook!

For a complete listing of all my books please see my author page.

INTRODUCTION

Welcome to *The Effortless Chef Series*! Thank you for taking the time to download the *Easy Irish Cookbook*. Come take a journey with me into the delights of easy cooking. The point of this cookbook and all my cookbooks is to exemplify the effortless nature of cooking simply.

In this book we focus on the food of Ireland. You will find that even though the recipes are simple, the taste of the dishes is quite amazing.

So will you join me in an adventure of simple cooking? If the answer is yes (and I hope it is) please consult the table of contents to find the dishes you are most interested in. Once you are ready jump right in and start cooking.

— Chef Maggie Chow

TABLE OF CONTENTS

ANY ISSUES? CONTACT ME

If you find that something important to you is missing from this book please contact me at maggie@booksumo.com.

I will try my best to re-publish a revised copy taking your feedback into consideration and let you know when the book has been revised with you in mind.

:)

— Chef Maggie Chow

LEGAL NOTES

Common Abbreviations

cup(s)	C.
tablespoon	tbsp
teaspoon	tsp
ounce	oz.
pound	lb

*All units used are standard American measurements

Chapter 1: Easy Irish Recipes

Beef Hash

Ingredients

- 2 tbsps butter
- 2 tbsps extra-virgin olive oil
- 1 large onion, diced
- 5 large Yukon Gold potatoes, peeled and cut into 1/4-inch cubes
- 1 large carrot, coarsely shredded
- 2 lbs cooked corned beef, cubed
- 2 tbsps diced fresh parsley
- 1/4 tsp dried thyme leaves
- salt to taste (optional)
- 1/2 tsp ground black pepper, or to taste

Directions

- Stir fry your onions in melted butter for 19 mins.
- Now combine in your carrots and potatoes. Cook everything for 16 more mins. Stir the mix every 5 mins.
- Add some pepper, thyme, salt, parsley, and your corned beef.
- Cook for another 16 mins with a medium to low heating level.
- Enjoy.

Amount per serving (8 total)

Timing Information:

Preparation	Cooking	Total Time
30 m	40 m	1 h 10 m

Nutritional Information:

Calories	320 kcal
Fat	14.1 g
Carbohydrates	24.6g
Protein	24.7 g
Cholesterol	81 mg
Sodium	1608 mg

* Percent Daily Values are based on a 2,000 calorie diet.

IRISH STEW I

(TOMATO, CARROTS, AND BEEF)

Ingredients

- 2 lbs lean beef stew meat, cut into 1-inch cubes
- 3 tbsps vegetable oil, divided
- 2 tbsps all-purpose flour
- 1 pinch salt and ground black pepper to taste
- 1 pinch cayenne pepper
- 2 large onions, diced
- 1 clove garlic, crushed
- 2 tbsps tomato paste
- 1 1/2 C. beer
- 2 C. diced carrot
- 1 sprig fresh thyme
- 1 tbsp diced fresh parsley for garnish

Directions

- Get a bowl combine: veggie oil (1 tbsp) and beef cubes. Coat them evenly.
- Get a 2nd bowl, mix: cayenne, flour, pepper, and salt.
- Combine both bowls, and make sure all the beef pieces are coated.
- Fry your beef in the remaining oil in a large pot or Dutch oven. Then add your garlic, onions, tomato paste, and some water. Place a lid on the pot and let the contents simmer for about 7 mins with a lower level of heat.
- Take half of your beef and add it to the stew and get it boiling. Stir everything nicely. Add your carrots, the remaining beef and beer, and thyme. Place a lid on the pot and set the heat to a very low level and let everything lightly boil for about 1.5 hours. Stir the stew every 35 mins.
- Add some salt for your own tastes.
- Top the dish with some fresh parsley before serving.

- Enjoy.

Amount per serving (6 total)

Timing Information:

Preparation	Cooking	Total Time
30 m	3 h	3 h 30 m

Nutritional Information:

Calories	518 kcal
Fat	36.1 g
Carbohydrates	14.2g
Protein	29.4 g
Cholesterol	101 mg
Sodium	160 mg

* Percent Daily Values are based on a 2,000 calorie diet.

Cabbage, Potatoes, and Leeks

Ingredients

- 1 lb cabbage
- 1 lb potatoes
- 2 leeks
- 1 C. milk
- salt and pepper to taste
- 1 pinch ground mace
- 1/2 C. butter

Directions

- Boil your cabbage until it is soft. Then boil your potatoes until they are soft as well. Remove all the remaining liquid and shut off the heat.
- Cut up all your leeks and then lightly boil them in milk until tender.

- Add some salt to your potatoes then mash them and add in your milk and leeks.
- Add the cabbage and warm the mix until it is a light green color.
- Finally mix in your butter and enjoy.

Amount per serving (5 total)

Timing Information:

Preparation	Cooking	Total Time
10 m	50 m	1 h 10 m

Nutritional Information:

Calories	302 kcal
Fat	19.7 g
Carbohydrates	28.6g
Protein	5.3 g
Cholesterol	53 mg
Sodium	180 mg

* Percent Daily Values are based on a 2,000 calorie diet.

Irish Stew II

(Bacon, Beef, and Beer)

Ingredients

- 6 slices bacon, diced
- 1/3 C. all-purpose flour
- 1 tsp salt
- 1/2 tsp ground black pepper
- 1 tsp ground allspice
- 2 1/2 lbs cubed beef stew meat
- 4 carrots, peeled and cut diagonally into 1-inch pieces
- 4 large onions, cut into eighths
- 2 cloves garlic, diced
- 1/4 C. minced fresh parsley
- 1 tsp dried rosemary, crushed
- 1 tsp dried marjoram
- 1 bay leaf
- 1 (12 fluid oz.) can beer

Directions

- Fry your bacon then set it to the side for later. Keep the fat in the pan.
- Get a resealable bag and in it add: allspice, flour, beef, pepper, and salt. Shake to coat the beef evenly.
- Fry your beef in the bacon fat until fully cooked. Put the beef in your slow cooker, and combine in: bay leaves, carrots, marjoram, onions, rosemary, onions, parsley, and garlic.
- Now boil your beer in the pan you fried your bacon in. Then pour the beer into the crock pot as well.
- Place a lid on your slow cooker and cook the stew on medium for 5 hrs until everything is nice and soft.
- Garnish the stew with your bacon.
- Enjoy.

Amount per serving (6 total)

Timing Information:

Preparation	Cooking	Total Time
10 m	5 h 10 m	5 h 20 m

Nutritional Information:

Calories	576 kcal
Fat	38.5 g
Carbohydrates	19.7g
Protein	36.4 g
Cholesterol	123 mg
Sodium	729 mg

* Percent Daily Values are based on a 2,000 calorie diet.

Irish Stew III

(Bacon, Beef, and Beer)

Ingredients

- 1 tbsp olive oil
- 2 lbs boneless lamb shoulder, cut into 1 1/2 inch pieces
- 1/2 tsp salt
- freshly ground black pepper to taste
- 1 large onion, sliced
- 2 carrots, peeled and cut into large chunks
- 1 parsnip, peeled and cut into large chunks (optional)
- 4 C. water, or as needed
- 3 large potatoes, peeled and quartered
- 1 tbsp diced fresh rosemary (optional)
- 1 C. coarsely diced leeks
- diced fresh parsley for garnish (optional)

Directions

- Fry your lamb in oil in a Dutch oven. Then add in your pepper and salt.
- Now combine in your parsnips, carrots and onions. Cook for 2 mins. Then add water.
- Place a lid on the pot and bring the contents to a boil before setting the heat to low and then simmering for 1 hr and 10 mins. Make sure that after the simmering time your lamb is soft.
- Add your potatoes and continue lightly boiling the stew for 20 mins.
- Then add the rosemary and leeks.
- Remove the lid from the pot and let the potatoes cook until soft.
- When serving the dish top it with some fresh parsley.
- Enjoy.

Amount per serving (6 total)

Timing Information:

Preparation	Cooking	Total Time
15 m	1 h 45 m	2 h

Nutritional Information:

Calories	609 kcal
Fat	35.1 g
Carbohydrates	43.4g
Protein	29.8 g
Cholesterol	109 mg
Sodium	325 mg

* Percent Daily Values are based on a 2,000 calorie diet.

Irish Pot Pie

Ingredients

- 1 pastry for a 9 inch single crust pie
- 1 (4 lb) whole chicken, deboned and cut into bite size pieces
- 4 slices cooked ham
- 4 leeks, diced
- 1 onion, diced
- salt and pepper to taste
- 1 pinch ground mace
- 1 1/4 C. chicken stock
- 1 tbsp milk
- 1/2 C. heavy cream

Directions

- Set your oven to 350 degrees before doing anything else.
- Layer the following in a baking dish: ham, onions, leeks, and chicken.

- Continue layering until ingredients are used. Between each layer add some mace, pepper, and salt.
- Pour in your stock around the layers.
- Cover the top of the casserole with your pastry after you have flattened it. Cut the edge of the pastry to that it fits nicely around the dish. Coat the top of the pastry with some milk.
- Cook the pie in the oven for 45 mins.
- Warm your cream on the stove and top the casserole with cream when serving.
- Enjoy.

Amount per serving (6 total)

Timing Information:

Preparation	Cooking	Total Time
40 m	35 m	1 h 15 m

Nutritional Information:

Calories	599 kcal
Fat	32.5 g
Carbohydrates	24.8g
Protein	49.6 g
Cholesterol	166 mg
Sodium	755 mg

* Percent Daily Values are based on a 2,000 calorie diet.

Irish Stew IV

(Creamy Dumplings and Chicken)

Ingredients

- 2 (10.75 oz.) cans condensed cream of chicken soup
- 3 C. water
- 1 C. diced celery
- 2 onions, quartered
- 1 tsp salt
- 1/2 tsp poultry seasoning
- 1/2 tsp ground black pepper
- 4 skinless, boneless chicken breast halves
- 5 carrots, sliced
- 1 (10 oz.) package frozen green peas
- 4 potatoes, quartered
- 3 C. baking mix
- 1 1/3 C. milk

Directions

- Combine the following in a Dutch oven: pepper, soup, poultry seasoning, water, salt, chicken, onions, and celery.
- Place a lid on the pot and simmer after boiling with a low heat for 1 hr and 45 mins.
- Combine in your carrots and then the potatoes and continue simmering for 35 more mins.
- Take out the chicken from the mix and shred it with a large fork and then put the meat back in the pot.
- Add in your peas and let the peas cook for 6 more mins.
- Get a bowl and combine milk and baking mix to make dough.
- Take spoonfuls of the dough and put them into the soup while it is simmering (to form dumplings).
- After you have entered all the dough into the soup.
- Let everything lightly boil with a lid on the pot for 13 mins.

- Then remove the lid and let the contents cook for 7 more mins.
- Enjoy.

Amount per serving (6 total)

Timing Information:

Preparation	Cooking	Total Time
20 m	2 h 40 m	3 h

Nutritional Information:

Calories	94.4g
Fat	9.2 g
Carbohydrates	94.4g
Protein	33.9 g
Cholesterol	58 mg
Sodium	2402 mg

* Percent Daily Values are based on a 2,000 calorie diet.

BEER BRISKET

Ingredients

- 4 lbs corned beef brisket
- 1 C. brown sugar
- 1 (12 fluid oz.) can stout beer

Directions

- Set your oven to 300 degrees before doing anything else.
- Clean your beef with water and then coat it with brown sugar. Put the beef in a Dutch oven and then pour the beer on top of it. Place a lid on the pot and cook it in the oven for 1 hr and 45 mins.
- Cut up your beef after it has sat for 10 mins outside the oven.
- Enjoy.

Amount per serving (16 total)

Timing Information:

Preparation	Cooking	Total Time
20 m	2 h 30 m	2 h 50 m

Nutritional Information:

Calories	277 kcal
Fat	16.9 g
Carbohydrates	13.6g
Protein	16.7 g
Cholesterol	61 mg
Sodium	1384 mg

* Percent Daily Values are based on a 2,000 calorie diet.

Potatoes, Leeks, and Cabbage II

Ingredients

- 2 1/2 lbs potatoes, peeled and cubed
- 4 slices bacon
- 1/2 small head cabbage, diced
- 1 large onion, diced
- 1/2 C. milk
- salt and pepper to taste
- 1/4 C. butter, melted

Directions

- Cover your potatoes in water and then boil; them for 22 mins. Remove all the water.
- Add in your milk and mash the potatoes. Then finally season the mash with some pepper and salt.
- Fry your bacon in a separate pan and then save the liquid fat, and

break apart the bacon. Place everything to the side.

- Cook your onions and cabbage in the bacon fat.
- Mix the onions and cabbage once they have finished cooking with the mashes potatoes.
- Put everything in a serving bowl and then add in your melted butter and mix everything evenly.
- Enjoy.

Amount per serving (8 total)

Timing Information:

Preparation	Cooking	Total Time
20 m	20 m	40 m

Nutritional Information:

Calories	250 kcal
Fat	12.6 g
Carbohydrates	29.8g
Protein	5.8 g
Cholesterol	26 mg
Sodium	217 mg

* Percent Daily Values are based on a 2,000 calorie diet.

STEWED CABBAGE

Ingredients

- 2 tsps butter
- 1 (15 oz.) can chicken broth
- 1 head cabbage, cored and coarsely diced
- 1 pinch salt and pepper to taste

Directions

- Boil your broth and butter in a pan and once boiling add in your cabbage. Lower the heat and then place a lid on the pan. Let the cabbage cook for 50 mins. Stir the contents every 10 mins. Add your pepper and salt.
- Enjoy hot.

Amount per serving (6 total)

Timing Information:

Preparation	Cooking	Total Time
5 m	45 m	50 m

Nutritional Information:

Calories	66 kcal
Fat	1.7 g
Carbohydrates	11.8g
Protein	2.9 g
Cholesterol	5 mg
Sodium	449 mg

* Percent Daily Values are based on a 2,000 calorie diet.

Apricot Irish Beef

Ingredients

- 4 1/2 lbs corned beef, rinsed
- 1 C. water
- 1 C. apricot preserves
- 1/4 C. brown sugar
- 2 tbsps soy sauce

Directions

- Set your oven to 350 degrees before doing anything else.
- Fry your corned beef in a pan with nonstick spray for 2 mins. Then add in your water.
- Place a lid on the pan or a covering of foil and cook it in the oven for 2 hrs. Then remove all the liquid.
- Get a bowl, and mix: soy sauce, apricot preserves, and brown sugar.

- Coat your beef with this mix.
- Continue cooking the beef in the oven for 35 more mins. Baste the beef every 10 mins.
- Cut the beef into pieces before serving, after it has cooled off a bit.
- Enjoy.

Amount per serving (7 total)

Timing Information:

Preparation	Cooking	Total Time
15 m	3 h	3 h 15 m

Nutritional Information:

Calories	463 kcal
Fat	24.3 g
Carbohydrates	38.1g
Protein	23.8 g
Cholesterol	125 mg
Sodium	1725 mg

* Percent Daily Values are based on a 2,000 calorie diet.

PEPPER BRISKET AND POTATOES

Ingredients

- 4 1/2 lbs corned beef brisket
- 5 black peppercorns
- 1/2 tsp garlic powder
- 1 onion, peeled and left whole
- 2 bay leaves
- 1 pinch salt
- 1 small head cabbage, cored and cut into wedges
- 6 large potatoes, quartered
- 4 large carrots, peeled and sliced
- 1/4 C. diced fresh parsley
- 2 tbsps butter

Directions

- Add your beef to a Dutch oven. Then add the following seasonings: salt, peppercorns, onions, and garlic powder.

- Cover everything with enough water and get the contents boiling. Let the beef boil for 23 mins. Remove any floating contents from the boiling as the meat cooks.
- After 23 mins has elapsed set the heat to low and let everything lightly boil for 3 more hrs.
- Now add your carrots, potatoes, and cabbage. Let the contents cook for 20 more mins. Now add the butter and shut off the heat.
- Take out your meat and let it sit for 20 mins, and put your veggies in a separate dish or bowl.
- Cut up your meat and then enjoy with the warm veggies.

Amount per serving (8 total)

Timing Information:

Preparation	Cooking	Total Time
20 m	3 h	3 h 20 m

Nutritional Information:

Calories	515 kcal
Fat	24.4 g
Carbohydrates	49.2g
Protein	25.5 g
Cholesterol	117 mg
Sodium	1377 mg

* Percent Daily Values are based on a 2,000 calorie diet.

Cocktail Beef

Ingredients

- 2 lbs cubed stew meat
- 6 carrots, diced
- 2 onions, diced
- 2 C. cubed potatoes
- 1 tbsp brown sugar
- 3 tbsps tapioca flour
- 1 C. tomato-vegetable juice cocktail

Directions

- Set your oven to 250 degrees before doing anything else.
- Get a big pot and enter in it: potatoes, meat, onions, and carrots.
- Get a bowl, mix: cocktail juice, sugar, and flour.
- Top the veggies and meat with the bowl contents. And simply

cook everything in the oven for 5 hrs.

- Enjoy.

Amount per serving (12 total)

Timing Information:

Preparation	Cooking	Total Time
10 m	5 h	5 h 10 m

Nutritional Information:

Calories	246 kcal
Fat	14.7 g
Carbohydrates	13.3g
Protein	15 g
Cholesterol	51 mg
Sodium	124 mg

* Percent Daily Values are based on a 2,000 calorie diet.

Apple Cabbage and Beef

Ingredients

- 1 (5 1/2 lb) corned beef brisket
- 2 tbsps pickling spice
- 1 large orange, sliced in rounds
- 2 stalks celery, sliced
- 1 large onion, sliced
- 1/2 C. cold water
- 6 tbsps margarine, divided
- 1 large head cabbage, cored and sliced
- 1 C. Golden Delicious apples, cored and quartered with peel
- 1/4 C. cold water

Directions

- Set your oven to 300 degrees before doing anything else.
- Get a baking dish and line it with foil. Make sure to use enough foil so that you can wrap the foil

around the contents inside the dish later.

- Clean your beef with water and then enter it into the pan.
- Coat the meat with the pickling spice.
- Then put the following around the beef: onions, orange, and celery. Then add half a C. of water to the dish and cover everything with the foil. Cook this in the oven for 4 hrs.
- Get a pan and heat one fourth of a C. of water and 3 tbsps of margarine. Then add your peas, and cabbage. Place a lid on the pan and let the contents simmer for 35 mins.
- After slicing up your beef top it with the apple and cabbage mix.
- Enjoy.

Amount per serving (8 total)

Timing Information:

Preparation	Cooking	Total Time
15 m	4 h	4 h 15 m

Nutritional Information:

Calories	482 kcal
Fat	34.1 g
Carbohydrates	16.9g
Protein	27.5 g
Cholesterol	134 mg
Sodium	1680 mg

* Percent Daily Values are based on a 2,000 calorie diet.

Lamb & Potato Pot Pie

Ingredients

- 1 tbsp olive oil
- 1 tbsp butter
- 1 onion, diced
- 2 lbs lean ground lamb
- 1/3 C. all-purpose flour
- salt and ground black pepper to taste
- 2 tsps minced fresh rosemary
- 1 tsp paprika
- 1/8 tsp ground cinnamon
- 1 tbsp ketchup
- 3 cloves garlic, minced
- 2 1/2 C. water, or as needed
- 1 (12 oz.) package frozen peas and carrots, thawed
- 2 1/2 lbs Yukon Gold potatoes, peeled and halved
- 1 tbsp butter
- 1 pinch ground cayenne pepper
- 1/4 C. cream cheese
- 1/4 lb Irish cheese, shredded

- salt and ground black pepper to taste
- 1 egg yolk
- 2 tbsps milk

Directions

- Set your oven to 375 degrees before doing anything else.
- Stir fry your onions and lamb in butter and olive oil for 12 mins in a Dutch oven. Then break up the lamb.
- Then add the following to your lamb: garlic, flour, ketchup, salt, cinnamon, pepper, paprika, and rosemary. Cook for 4 more mins.
- Add in your water and get everything boiling. Once boiling, lower the heat so everything is only lightly boiling and then let the contents go for 7 mins.
- Shut off the heat and add your carrots and peas.
- Pour everything into a casserole dish.

- Boil the potatoes in salt and water for 17 mins.
- Remove all the liquid.
- Now mash your potatoes with: Irish cheese, butter, cream cheese, and cayenne. Finally add your preferred amount of pepper and salt.
- Get a bowl, mix: milk and egg yolks.
- Then combine with the potatoes.
- Enter the potatoes with the lamb in the casserole dish.
- Cook everything in the oven for 35 mins.
- Enjoy after letting the dish sit for 5 mins.

Amount per serving (10 total)

Timing Information:

Preparation	Cooking	Total Time
25 m	1 h 10 m	1 h 35 m

Nutritional Information:

Calories	413 kcal
Fat	22.6 g
Carbohydrates	29.8g
Protein	23.3 g
Cholesterol	106 mg
Sodium	210 mg

* Percent Daily Values are based on a 2,000 calorie diet.

Bacon, Potato, Soup

Ingredients

- 1/2 lb Irish bacon, diced
- 2 large potatoes, peeled and cubed
- 1 (15 oz.) can diced tomatoes with juice
- 1 C. chicken stock, or as needed
- Salt and black pepper to taste
- 2 C. thinly sliced dark green Savoy cabbage leaves

Directions

- Cook your bacon in a big pot then remove any excess oils. Add your tomatoes, potatoes and stock. Add in your pepper and salt and get everything boiling.
- Once the mix is boiling, lower the heat and let the contents cook for 22 mins.

- Add the cabbage after 22 mins of simmering and let the contents keep cooking for 5 more mins.
- Enjoy.

Amount per serving (4 total)

Timing Information:

Preparation	Cooking	Total Time
15 m	30 m	45 m

Nutritional Information:

Calories	276 kcal
Fat	8.1 g
Carbohydrates	38.4g
Protein	12.3 g
Cholesterol	21 mg
Sodium	825 mg

* Percent Daily Values are based on a 2,000 calorie diet.

Irish Turkey Pot Pie

Ingredients

- cooking spray
- 1 1/2 lbs russet potatoes, peeled and cut into 1 1/2-inch thick slices
- 6 tbsps butter, cut into pieces
- 1 C. milk
- salt and pepper, to taste
- 1 tbsp vegetable oil
- 1 lb ground turkey
- 1 medium onion, diced
- 2 (1 oz.) packages instant chicken gravy mix
- 1 C. water
- 1 (16 oz.) package frozen peas and carrots, thawed
- 2 C. shredded cheese, your preferred type

Directions

- Coat a casserole dish with nonstick spray or oil then set your oven to 350 degrees before doing anything else.
- Boil your potatoes for 30 mins and then remove all liquids and mash them.
- Add in with the potatoes: pepper, butter, salt, and milk. Mash the potatoes again to mix everything in.
- Stir fry your onions and turkey in 1 tbsp of oil until the turkey is cooked.
- Combine with the turkey your water and gravy the pepper and salt.
- Heat the gravy until simmering. Let the gravy simmer until it nice and thick.
- Put the turkey in the casserole dish then add in your carrots and peas, and finally cover everything with your potatoes.
- The final layer should be cheese.
- Cook the dish in the oven for 30 mins.

- Enjoy after letting the casserole sit for 10 mins.

Amount per serving (6 total)

Timing Information:

Preparation	Cooking	Total Time
30 m	50 m	1 h 20 m

Nutritional Information:

Calories	566 kcal
Fat	34.4 g
Carbohydrates	36g
Protein	30.5 g
Cholesterol	130 mg
Sodium	1036 mg

* Percent Daily Values are based on a 2,000 calorie diet.

Maggie's Favorite Irish Soup

Ingredients

- 18 small red new potatoes
- 6 C. chicken broth
- 3 leeks, diced
- 3 tbsps butter
- 2 C. milk
- salt and pepper to taste

Directions

- Boil your potatoes until they are soft.
- While the potatoes are boiling fry your leeks in butter until they are see through.
- After the potatoes are finished remove all their skins and chunk them. Remove all the liquid from the pot and put the potatoes back

in the pot with the broth and your fried leeks.

- Add in some pepper and salt then simmer everything for 6 mins.
- Now add the milk and simmer everything another 5 mins.
- Enjoy hot.

Amount per serving (8 total)

Timing Information:

Preparation	Cooking	Total Time
30 m	45 m	1 h 30 m

Nutritional Information:

Calories	400 kcal
Fat	6.3 g
Carbohydrates	77.6g
Protein	9.7 g
Cholesterol	20 mg
Sodium	796 mg

* Percent Daily Values are based on a 2,000 calorie diet.

Steaks from Ireland

Ingredients

- 2 tbsps vegetable oil
- 3 tbsps butter
- 1 onion, diced
- 4 (4 oz.) beef top sirloin steaks
- 1 clove garlic, cut in half lengthwise
- 1/4 C. Irish whiskey (such as Jameson(R))
- salt and ground black pepper to taste
- 2 tbsps diced fresh flat-leaf parsley

Directions

- Stir fry your onions in butter and veggie oil for 12 mins. Fry your steaks in the same pan after rubbing them with the cut cloves of garlic.

- Cook the steak for 3 mins on each side.
- Shut off the heat.
- Add in the whiskey and take care to not cause any fires.
- Get everything lightly boiling and add in: parsley, pepper, and salt. Let the whiskey cook down a bit.
- Enjoy your steak with a topping of more cooked whiskey.

Amount per serving (4 total)

Timing Information:

Preparation	Cooking	Total Time
15 m	15 m	30 m

Nutritional Information:

Calories	363 kcal
Fat	25 g
Carbohydrates	5.7g
Protein	19.7 g
Cholesterol	83 mg
Sodium	107 mg

* Percent Daily Values are based on a 2,000 calorie diet.

Mushroom and Beef Pot Pie

Ingredients

- 3 tbsps olive oil, divided
- 1 lb cubed beef stew meat
- 2 slices bacon, diced
- 1 white onion, diced
- 1 carrot, sliced
- 1/3 lb crimini mushrooms, sliced
- 1 clove garlic, crushed
- 1 tsp white sugar
- 1 1/2 tbsps all-purpose flour
- 1 C. Irish beer
- 1 1/4 C. beef stock
- 1/2 tsp ground thyme
- 2 bay leaves
- 1/2 tsp cornstarch, or as needed
- 1 tsp water
- 1 sheet frozen puff pastry, thawed
- 1 egg, beaten

Directions

- Fry your beef in 2 tbsps of olive oil for 12 mins. Then place everything to the side.
- Fry your bacon in 1 tbsp of olive oil for a few mins and then add in sugar, onions, garlic, mushrooms, and carrots. Stir fry everything for 16 mins until tender.
- Add in your flour and mix evenly. Then slowly add in the stock and beer.
- Once the stock and beer has been incorporated. Add the bay leaves, and thyme.
- Get everything boiling then place a lid on the pan and lower the heat.
- Let the contents lightly boil for 1 hr and 20 mins.
- Then take off the lid and let everything keep boiling for 20 more mins to thicken the sauce.
- Add your cornstarch and water and let everything simmer for 32 mins.

- After 15 mins of simmering set your oven to 350 degrees before doing anything else.
- Line a pie dish with puff pastry and fill the pie with the stew.
- Cover the stew with more puff pastry.
- Seal the edges with a utensil (large fork) and then cut some openings into the pie. Top with whisked eggs. Cook in the oven for 40 mins.
- Enjoy.

Amount per serving (6 total)

Timing Information:

Preparation	Cooking	Total Time
25 m	2 h 35 m	3 h

Nutritional Information:

Calories	500 kcal
Fat	31.7 g
Carbohydrates	28.6g
Protein	21.8 g
Cholesterol	77 mg
Sodium	259 mg

* Percent Daily Values are based on a 2,000 calorie diet.

Dinner in Ireland

Ingredients

- 3 lbs smoked pork shoulder
- salt and pepper to taste
- 2 large onions, quartered
- 6 potatoes, peeled
- 8 oz. carrots, cut in half
- 1 large head cabbage, quartered
- 1 lb fresh green beans, trimmed

Directions

- Boil your pork in a big pot in water with pepper and salt. Place a lid on the pot. Once the pork is boiling set the heat to low and cook for 35 mins.
- Mix in your onions, carrots, beans, cabbage, and potatoes.
- Keep cooking everything for about 30 mins until all the veggies are soft.

- Plate your pork on a serving dish and put the veggies around it.
- Enjoy the meal after it has sat for about 13 mins.

Amount per serving (6 total)

Timing Information:

Preparation	Cooking	Total Time
15 m	55 m	1 h 20 m

Nutritional Information:

Calories	753 kcal
Fat	40.6 g
Carbohydrates	63.5g
Protein	38.4 g
Cholesterol	130 mg
Sodium	2715 mg

* Percent Daily Values are based on a 2,000 calorie diet.

Easy Corned Beef

Ingredients

- 1 1/2 lbs potatoes, peeled and quartered
- 1 1/2 lbs cooked corned beef, finely diced
- 1 bunch green onions, diced
- salt and ground black pepper to taste
- 2 cloves garlic, crushed
- 1 tbsp butter
- 1/4 C. roasted tomato salsa

Directions

- Boil your potatoes in salt and water. Once boiling place a lid on the pot and let it cook for 17 mins. Then remove all liquid and dice them in little cubes for hash.
- Fry your beef in a frying pan until it begins to render some fat.

- Then add in your onions, garlic, butter, pepper, and salt.
- Fry everything for about 2 mins. Add in your potatoes, some more salt, and some salsa to the mix.
- Split the mix into 4 parts.
- Cook for 5 mins until the bottom begins to get a bit hard. Then turn over the hash and cook another 5 mins.
- Continue frying and turning each section for about 15 to 17 mins turning over the mix every 5 mins.
- Enjoy.

Amount per serving (4 total)

Timing Information:

Preparation	Cooking	Total Time
15 m	35 m	50 m

Nutritional Information:

Calories	608 kcal
Fat	35.5 g
Carbohydrates	36.2g
Protein	35.8 g
Cholesterol	174 mg
Sodium	2068 mg

* Percent Daily Values are based on a 2,000 calorie diet.

EASY POTATO AND PEPPERS

Ingredients

- 6 large russet (baking) potatoes
- 1 large green bell pepper, cut into 1/2-inch dice
- 1 large red bell pepper, cut into 1/2-inch dice
- 1 large onion, cut into 1/2-inch dice
- 1/4 C. vegetable oil

Directions

- Boil your potatoes in water and salt. Once boiling place a lid on the pot and set the heat to low and let the contents cook for 12 mins.
- Remove the liquid and let the potatoes lose all of their heat. Dice up these potatoes before doing anything else.

- Get a bowl, combine: onions, diced potatoes, green and red bell peppers, and veggie oil.
- Divide the potatoes and peppers amongst multiple resealable plastic bags and keep them in the freezer.
- To cook this mix. You want to fry them in a frying pan coated with nonstick spray for about 20 mins with a low to medium level of heat. While cooking stir every 5 mins.
- Enjoy.

Amount per serving (8 total)

Timing Information:

Preparation	Cooking	Total Time
15 m	30 m	1 h 15 m

Nutritional Information:

Calories	291 kcal
Fat	7.2 g
Carbohydrates	52.3g
Protein	6.2 g
Cholesterol	0 mg
Sodium	19 mg

* Percent Daily Values are based on a 2,000 calorie diet.

Butter Potatoes

Ingredients

- 8 large russet potatoes
- 1 tbsp butter
- 1/2 small onion, minced
- salt and ground black pepper to taste
- 1/2 C. butter, melted
- 1/2 C. heavy whipping cream
- 1/2 C. half-and-half
- 1/4 tsp paprika (optional)
- 2 tbsps diced fresh parsley (optional)

Directions

- Boil your potatoes in salt and water for 13 mins. Then remove all liquid and allow them to cool. Then remove the skins and place them in the fridge for 1 and a half hours.

- Now you want to grate the potatoes and place them in a bowl.
- Set your oven to 350 degrees before doing anything else. Coat a casserole dish with oil or nonstick spray.
- Layer the following into your dish: grated potatoes, salt and pepper, and then one fourth of the onions. Continue layering in this manner until all the potatoes are used.
- Top with some half and half, whipping cream, and melted butter. Finally with paprika.
- Cook in the oven for 35 mins.
- Before serving garnish with fresh parsley.
- Enjoy.

Amount per serving (8 total)

Timing Information:

Preparation	Cooking	Total Time
20 m	40 m	2 h

Nutritional Information:

Calories	448 kcal
Fat	17.8 g
Carbohydrates	67.8g
Protein	6.5 g
Cholesterol	50 mg
Sodium	167 mg

* Percent Daily Values are based on a 2,000 calorie diet.

Full Irish Breakfast

Ingredients

- 2 thick slices bacon
- 2 sausages
- 1 soda bread farl, sliced in half horizontally
- 2 potato bread farls
- 1 tbsp vegetable oil, or as needed
- 2 slices black pudding
- 1 tomato, halved
- 2 eggs

Directions

- Set your oven to 300 degrees before doing anything else.
- Stir fry you sausage and bacon and once finished place then in a baking dish and then the oven.
- Keep the drippings from the bacon and sausage in a pan. Cook

your soda farls and potatoes in this pan until golden.

- In another pan fry your tomato halves and black pudding slices in hot oil for 3 mins. Then put them in the oven with sausage and bacon.
- Break your eggs in the pan with the grease and fry them for a few mins until the whites get hard the yolks are still runny.
- Plate the eggs and the contents in the oven for two people.
- Enjoy.

Amount per serving (2 total)

Timing Information:

Preparation	Cooking	Total Time
5 m	25 m	30 m

Nutritional Information:

Calories	643 kcal
Fat	47.7 g
Carbohydrates	32.4g
Protein	21 g
Cholesterol	227 mg
Sodium	957 mg

* Percent Daily Values are based on a 2,000 calorie diet.

ORZO, LEEKS, AND SHERRY SOUP

Ingredients

- 4 oz. fresh mushrooms, sliced
- 1 C. sliced leeks
- 2 tbsps margarine
- 2 tbsps olive oil
- 1/2 C. dry sherry
- 3 (10.5 oz.) cans condensed beef broth
- 3 3/4 C. water
- 1/2 tsp ground black pepper
- 1/2 C. uncooked orzo pasta

Directions

- Fry your leeks and mushrooms in olive oil until they are soft. Then pour in your sherry and simmer the liquid until half of it evaporates.

- Combine your pepper, broth, and water. Get everything boiling. Once boiling, mix in your orzo.
- Let the contents boil for 13 mins.
- When serving the soup top with freshly sliced or diced mushrooms.
- Enjoy.

Amount per serving (6 total)

Timing Information:

Preparation	Cooking	Total Time
15 m	35 m	50 m

Nutritional Information:

Calories	182 kcal
Fat	8.4 g
Carbohydrates	19.6g
Protein	6.7 g
Cholesterol	6 mg
Sodium	1233 mg

* Percent Daily Values are based on a 2,000 calorie diet.

A Gift From Me To You...

Send the Book!

I know you like easy cooking. But what about Japanese Sushi?

Join my private reader's club and get a copy of ***Infinite Sushi: A Complete Set of Sushi and Japanese Recipes*** by fellow BookSumo author Hashimoto Kazuma for FREE!

Send the Book!

Enjoy some of the best sushi available!

You will also receive updates about all my new books when they are free. So please show your support.

Also don't forget to like and subscribe on the social networks. I love meeting my readers. Links to all my profiles are below so please click and connect :)

Facebook

Twitter

Come On...
Let's Be Friends :)

I adore my readers and love connecting with them socially. Please follow the links below so we can connect on Facebook, Twitter, and Google+.

Facebook

Twitter

I also have a blog that I regularly update for my readers so check it out below.

My Blog

Can I Ask A Favour?

If you found this book interesting, or have otherwise found any benefit in it. Then may I ask that you post a review of it on Amazon? Nothing excites me more than new reviews, especially reviews which suggest new topics for writing. I do read all reviews and I always factor feedback into my newer works.

So if you are willing to take ten minutes to write what you sincerely thought about this book then please visit our Amazon page and post your opinions.

Again thank you!

INTERESTED IN OTHER EASY COOKBOOKS?

Everything is easy! Check out my Amazon Author page for more great cookbooks:

For a complete listing of all my books please see my author page.

Made in United States
Orlando, FL
22 March 2022